HOW TO FORM A MASTERMIND ALLIANCE

Coordinate Knowledge and Effort in a Spirit of Harmony to Multiply Your Effectiveness and Produce Richer Results

by
Steve Anderson

with an introduction by
Walter Hailey

HOW TO FORM A MASTERMIND ALLIANCE
Coordinate knowledge and effort in a spirit of harmony to multiply your effectiveness and produce richer results.

Published by Planned Marketing, Inc., Hunt, Texas

For Ordering Information Call 1-800-HUNT-TEX

ISBN: 1-882-306-12-0

Printed in the United States of America

TABLE OF CONTENTS

To the hundreds of people who have shared their valuable time with me, helping me avoid the many mistakes I would surely have made had I never been given the chance to benefit from their counsel.

INTRODUCTION

BY WALTER HAILEY

The Master Mind Alliance is an emperor of an idea in a kingdom of powerful concepts which have brought me great riches and enormous personal happiness. It's been with me from the very beginning of my life and it's how I got where I am today, including how I found Steve Anderson, the President of Planned Marketing Associates, the fullest embodiment of a Master Mind thinker I have ever met in my fifty years in business.

I ask the reader to indulge Ol' Grandpa Hailey and let me tell you the whole story, much as I might narrate it to my own grandkids. Besides, it's only appropriate; it was my grandma who introduced me to the Master Mind idea, though she didn't call it that at the time. In fact, it wasn't until I'd read Napoleon Hill's ***Think and Grow Rich*** that I formalized what she'd taught me to do all along. Hill called a Master Mind Alliance, *the coordination of knowledge and effort, in a spirit of harmony, between two or more people, for the attainment of a definite purpose.*

Though Hill's book changed my life, the greatest Master Mind Alliance I have ever had was with Grandma. She worshipped me. Good as my mom and dad had been to me, I knew Grandma was something special. Being the shortest kid in the history of Mesquite, Texas, was not easy on me. Whenever we chose up teams for baseball or football, I wanted to be first. But it was not to be. While the other guys had nicknames like Buck and Big Bob and Bubba, I got to be known as "Itsy Bitsy" Hailey. Watching from the sidelines, it was easy to become even smaller by thinking less of myself. Talk about low self-esteem. I couldn't lead a group in silent prayer! When they huddled up on the field, I thought they were talking about *me!*

Grandma brooked no tolerance for any form of self-pity, however. And she taught me something more important than hitting home runs and scoring touchdowns. She told me, "Bitsy, it don't make no difference how big you are in body. What's important is how big you are in mind."

So began my Master Mind training.

Though Grandma was no scholar or philosopher, when it came to teaching me what was right she had the instincts of a sage. And I had no barrier to learning from her. It was trust at first sight. And the trust grew. I might have been young in years and small in size, but she spoke to me as if I were a thinking person. So I became a thinking person. Of course, it wasn't until I got out in the world that I realized her homespun, non-denominational way of seeing contained pretty much the message of all the great religions all over the world. That truth is not the exclusive property of any one group is a great lesson in itself, but back then I only knew that she had succeeded in opening my mind to its infinite possibilities. She schooled me in such a way that even mystical things had a practical side to them. For example, she'd say to me, "Bitsy, you can't outgive the spirit. If you're lookin' to get rich, you'll find it in enrichin' others."

She also taught me that thought is magnetic. The conscious mind is only a small part of the entire mind. If you feed the mind positive things, you will tap into the universal mind and create a magnet for those things to come into your life. She'd say, "The human mind is a wonderful mystery, Bitsy. Remember that what you're lookin' for, is lookin' for you! What you want, wants you."

Perhaps her greatest impact on me was the feeling I had when I was around her. Everything seemed possible when we were together. Like they say, "Ain't no mountain high enough. . . ." I know now that the loving sensation we exchanged was the spirit of harmony at work. The French call it *rapport*; the Spanish call it *simpatico*; the Japanese call it *haragei*. It's a listening with the heart, the mind and the total body. I knew not to be afraid of this intimacy, that this was the foundation for achieving great things. And when she'd see me all messed up – selfish, angry and hanging back, all full of grudges and doubt – she'd tap me on the shoulder and say, "Bitsy, why don't you just leave your ego at the door and come on in here where it's warm and we can get something accomplished?"

My Master Mind training continued in the Boy Scouts. I flew right up to Eagle faster than anyone else in the state of Texas had ever done. But every night before bed, Grandma would ask me, "Bisty, what was the good turn you done today?" Those conversations revealed to me two things: the power in helping others and that happiness is not something to pursue in itself; happiness happens more like a side effect, a by-product of being fully human and useful to folks. The Boy Scout motto, "Be prepared," turned out to be pretty good advice, too.

My next Master Mind encounter was with the Future Farmers of America where I learned how to make money on a farm. I'd grown up on a farm and if there is one thing that ranching or farming will teach you, it's that you can't do it all by yourself. Cooperation is the only way to survive. Finding out what others need is the most crucial networking skill you can have. And all you have to do is ask. I learned a most valuable lesson when I learned to ASK.

My first job was nothing to write home about, but I managed to apply some of Grandma's wisdom. I was selling by myself and getting nowhere fast. So I met with seven other salespersons and we decided to show each other's products, in addition to our own, when we were making a presentation. We got to harmonize pretty well, covering each other's weaknesses and extending one another's strengths. At one point we brought a band along and soon we were doing eight store sales per week. We'd set up shop in the supermarket, give away some samples and multiply our results. It was synergy that we had created and we took it to the next level by learning how to work conventions and grocers' meetings.

But it wasn't until I got into the life insurance business that I really began to need all those Master Mind Alliance lessons that I'd enjoyed as a kid. And the reason was that I couldn't sell life insurance! You don't know rejection until you've been turned down by a pig farmer. So, while I was starving, I read. I stumbled upon Napoleon Hill's research. ***Think and Grow Rich*** was like manna from heaven. Suddenly I had a plan. I formed my first official Master Mind group. The Mesquite Nine met regularly in my living room. We set down goals. We *wrote* them down. We then began to help one another attain those goals. I'm happy to say that eight out of nine of us met the goals we had determined to meet.

The guy who didn't make it provided us with a valuable lesson, however: screen members for your Master Mind Alliance closely. Choose people who are of the same calibre of motivation. Beyond the obvious characteristics of loyalty, dependability and capability, make sure that each person adds a greater degree of harmony to the group.

It was harmony that turned out to be the most important quality in my next lesson in Master Minding. I'd always heard that opposites attract, but that didn't prepare me for David Keener. By this time I'd developed into quite the persuader: outgoing, people-loving, a bit impulsive, plenty of positive thinking. I was used to my *"can-do"* enthusiasm rubbing off on those around me. But he met my infectious style with a quiet scrutiny. I couldn't believe this guy. What is black and white to me became red for him. Talk about detail-oriented, David knew how to read not only the fine print but the information hidden between the lines. He was the marriage of magnificent wisdom and uncanny analytical ability.

We were made for each other. It was the first time I connected with someone who brought to the table an entirely different set of assets than I had. It began – and remained – a dynamic Master Mind. Like Napoleon Hill wrote, WHATEVER THE HUMAN MIND CAN CONCEIVE AND BELIEVE, IT CAN ACHIEVE.

In short, we built a business, using the NEER system. We used what was already working in the food industry. By buying together, independent corporations like A & P, Kroeger's and Safeway had managed to sell for less. The food cooperative links up supplier and customer, grower and grocer, consumer and manufacturer. We used this approach to sell business and personal insurance to grocers through their wholesalers. From one food warehouse in Dallas, we ended up expanding nationwide, ultimately insuring both the wholesalers' suppliers as well as their customers.

We also made use of a regular billing cycle, in which beans, peas and insurance were all on one bill. You can get the whole story in ***Breaking the NO Barrier***, but I'll just say here that David lent me a way of seeing and thinking and doing business that helped me break every record in the history of selling. I went from a 1 in 10 ratio of sales to calls to an 8 in 10. At one point I sold a million dollars of insurance in a month. Then a million in a week. Then a million in one day! As a company we sold one billion dollars in eight years.

Along with another Master Mind member, Mike Rabinowitz, we induced 800 K-Marts to buy insurance both for their stores and all their employees. We knew something this good had a price. We just didn't know what it might be. We didn't want it to end, but when

K-Mart offered us 78 million dollars, well – like the Godfather says, it was a deal we couldn't refuse.

Looking back, it wasn't that the ideas we used were revolutionary. It was the *application* of a couple of ideas that was revolutionary. After all, the invention of the computer was a great breakthrough, but it was the invention of the computer chip that made it possible for millions of people to own their own computers. And that's what has changed the world we live in more than the original idea. What we did together was nothing short of the Master Mind Alliance in action. *When two or more minds are hooked up in harmony, a third mind is formed, one only limited by the ability of those minds to work together to achieve a common purpose.*

In any case, I got out of the fast lane in Dallas and bought a ranch in the Texas Hill Country. I was not accustomed to sitting around and watching the paint dry, so when I discovered that a new tax law wanted 90% of my income, I called up some old friends with a business venture. I had met John Connally way back when he was the sales manager for Lyndon Johnson's radio station. I'd been selling radio advertising at the time to support myself through college. We stayed in touch and years later I ended up running John's successful campaign for governor of Texas. So, rather than lose our shirts in taxes, John, Ben Barnes, Dave Keener and I invested in oil. We sold our first stock at 80 cents a share. Within eighteen months, it was going for $9.50 a share. We had a great Master Mind Alliance and the company continued to grow. We recently sold it for $290 million.

Around this time, a neighbor with a weekend house, Dr. David McMahon, began to do a lot of visiting.

Together with the help of "insurance great" Jack Murphy, we ended up creating the country's leading doctor-owned malpractice insurance company. Using the same NEER marketing principles that had built the earlier businesses, we also took this company public, selling it for over $48 million.

Like a Hill Country rancher, I bought all this exotic game from Africa and South America. But after a while llamas and black buck antelope started to bore me. It was people I wanted to be with, people interested enough in their lives to commit themselves to making a difference. So I began to give seminars, first to folks in business and then to young people as well. For a guy like me, it was a perfect hobby.

About this time, I got a call from another Master Mind buddy who had been my roommate at the University of Texas. He needed help raising money to build a new chapter house for Sigma Phi Epsilon. As a young man I had thought fraternities were for rich kids, so I never joined one. But because I helped him with this project, I was made an honorary, 40-year-old-plus(!) pledge. Through the fraternity's national board, I was introduced to Steve Anderson, founder of the chapter at the University of Utah, who attended one of our early Boot Kamps.

At the end of it, he told me, "Hailey, I've learned more in three days than I've learned in my entire time in college. I'm going to form a Master Mind Alliance!"

What could I say? "That's great. Stay in touch."

What I didn't anticipate was the depth of his commitment to the idea. I found out later that he had ended up Master Minding with sixty of the top business minds in the country! Nor did I know, when he showed up a year later, diploma in hand, that he had been offered numerous positions with firms all over the country. All I knew was there he was, knocking on my door.

"How's that Master Mind Alliance going for you, Steve?"

"Hailey, I want to join *you*."

"You mean work for me? I got all the help I need."

"No, I don't mean help, I don't mean work for. I mean *join*. You've taken three companies public and that's what I want to do. I want to build a company with you and take it to Wall Street."

I still couldn't get it.

"What are you looking for, Steve, a salary?"

"I don't want a salary. Just pay me what I earn."

I'm a Depression-era baby so this wasn't exactly fitting into my world view. "Now hold on. Where will you live?"

"In that old guest house over there."

"All right," I told him, trying to stall, "go back to Utah and get your clothes."

"Hailey, my clothes are already in the car!"

Talk about being prepared (he's an Eagle Scout, too). He came prepared enough to not have to go back. And he's turned a hobby of mine into a multi-million dollar business.

Steve has taught an old dog like me some new tricks. The first is that Master Minding is not a switch you turn on and off. With Steve every minute is Master Mind time. It's not simply an attitude to bring to a business meeting; it's a state of mind, twenty-four hours a day, seven days a week. Like John Woods, one of our audio and video producers, says, "He understands that thinking is a pleasure.

That's why his mind is vast, even though he's young in years. His brain is always working."

He is of the new generation as well. By that, I mean he's not locked into a rigid identity. With me, he's a lot like David Keener: analytical, reflective, able to see the weaknesses in my plan, but never discouraging. With other team members, he's more the manager-of-the-future: quick to recognize and reward excellence; ready to challenge each to his or her next level; pleased to lead by example. With his wife, Cheryl, he's like a guy still on the honeymoon.

Another thing about Steve is that he has the gift of the poet in him. He can really surrender his own agenda and absorb the world around him. Articulate and empathetic, he knows instinctively that lesson Grandma was always teaching me: *leave your ego at the door and join the main event.*

He's the embodiment of what I'm trying to teach in Boot Kamp: **When two or more minds join with a common purpose in a spirit of harmony, there is nothing on earth that they cannot achieve together.**

THE SIX CORE CONCEPTS OF A MASTERMIND ALLIANCE

Although everything about the Master Mind Alliance involves the development of harmonious relationships with other people, the first step involves no one but yourself. You have to have a clear purpose and a vision for the future. It's impossible to help someone who doesn't know he or she needs help – or what kind of help. Eliminate all the distractions, drop the disguises, stop being ruled by external demands and simply confront your deepest truths.

It's here that you'll meet your other, secret self, the *you* who recognizes no defeat, no obstacle, no adversity. It is with this interior self that you'll do the most important Master Mind Alliancing in your life.

Everything that you'll achieve will be the direct result of your ability to connect with this source.

Once you have gone *directly to the core* of your own purpose in life, your motivation, desire and ambition, you will have already prepared the way for great things to happen. In the metaphor of the magnet that Walter's grandmother used, your mind will begin to magnetize the people and events that will bring your "meditation into action." Walter likes to call it, *a vivid vision which vibrates vibrantly*.

It is from such purposefulness that things happen.

Equally important, another realization begins to dawn on even the most self-reliant.

CORE CONCEPT #1:

You can't do it alone. To get from here to there, you need other people.

Something powerful happens when minds interact with trust and harmony. Wherever you turn for evidence, from Socrates and the idea of the Academy to the Founding Fathers and the Declaration of Independence, our history reveals one constant: *To achieve greatness, get a great team.*

Even the heroes of our popular mythologies and TV shows have a team. Superman has Lois Lane and Jimmy Olsen; Batman has Robin. Let's face it, even the Lone Ranger is not alone! He has Tonto – and Silver. And what does it take to make a great team? **The primary requirement for building a Master Mind Alliance is TRUST.**

Trust is that most basic human enzyme, the chemical building block for all social interaction. Although we are the dominant species on the planet, our newborns do not arrive in the world ready to fend for themselves. Unlike many animals, they require a long nurturing process to develop fully. Trust is the ultimate basis for that life-long work of becoming fully human.

CORE CONCEPT #2:
Trust

Your Master Mind Alliance is valuable only to the extent of the trust among its members. In reflecting on Walter's relationship with his grandmother, the idea that stands out most in my mind is his admission, "I had no barrier to learning from her. It was trust at first sight. And the trust grew."

In spite of the difference in age, they created a world without walls: no secrets, nothing withheld, and more importantly, a *willingness to disclose*, to say or do whatever would deepen the rapport. Such a willingness is not simply the gift of a child's innocence, but real trust in action. By exercising a *mutual degree of reciprocity,* we strengthen the bonds so that the burden of holding back is relaxed enough to allow a free flow of ideas. **With such a permission to be direct, spontaneous and honest, trust not only has a chance, it blossoms.**

When we realize that how the other person sees things is not a threat to our way of seeing things, we acknowledge the value of their perceptions. But when we actually experience the eyes of the other person seeing what we can't see, namely our backsides, we understand just how powerful the eyes of people we trust can be. It is from such trust that the third core concept arises.

CORE CONCEPT #3:
Harmony

From the motion of planets in outer space to the appearance of a well-dressed man or woman, from the running of a thriving business to the architecture which houses that business, from the music we choose to the food we eat, from the health of the human body to the complex functioning of the human mind, harmony rules. Organized knowledge itself is nothing but the harmony of facts, truths and natural law. Thinking is nothing but the successful harmony of a thousand different thoughts in orderly attainment toward a given direction. Leadership is nothing but the harmonious integration of the group's impulses in a way that satisfies everyone. Moreover, harmony in a social context – whether in a choir or symphony orchestra, whether in marriage or on an athletic field – remains the closest many human beings ever come to the sublimation of the personal ego for the larger good. *Little Me* becomes a powerful component of the *Big Us*.

In the same way that a sense of purpose leads to a willingness to work together, which creates a climate of trust, harmony deepens when everyone is aligned

100% with that common purpose. With no hidden agenda or ulterior motive, nothing can get in the way of where you're going—not ego or communication style or personal idiosyncracy, since everyone's got the group's best interest in mind all the time. Called *esprit de corps* by the French, it's the success behind all social partnerships. Analyze any fast growing company and three things will become immediately obvious: the people there love what they do; they care about what happens; and they recognize that there is more power in unity than in selfishness. Walter described it so well in relation to his grandmother when he said, "Perhaps her greatest impact on me was the feeling I had when I was around her. Everything seemed possible when we were together. I know now that the loving sensation we exchanged was the spirit of harmony at work. I knew not to be afraid of this intimacy, that this was the foundation for achieving great things."

CORE CONCEPT #4:

Out of the harmonious alliance of two or more minds, a third or additional mind, is created. That additional mind will last as long as the blending of the individual minds continues to exist. It will disintegrate the moment the trusting alliance ends.

This ability to bring together or blend different talents so that *something new gets created* is the secret of all Master Mind Alliances. If you bake a cake but leave out an essential ingredient, you'll still have a cake. When you taste it, however, you'll know that something is missing. And you can't ask for the salt or eggs or sugar or flour on the side. All the ingredients must mix. **For the most effective Master Minding to take place, a desire to blend is required.** More accurately, *a burning desire is necessary* since the essential elements involved will combust and undergo change.

When powerful human forces come together for a common purpose, a chemical transformation takes place in much the same way that two parts of hydrogen will join with one part of oxygen to create a new substance. As with water, the result is the creation of something new, neither hydrogen nor oxygen, **a whole which is greater than the sum of its parts.**

You know you are approaching a Master Mind Alliance when the following ingredients are present with another person: willingness and trust, a compelling common purpose, a burning desire to blend harmoniously, a recognition not only that you can't do it alone, but that "thought chemistry" makes of two human minds a third mind more powerful than the sum of its parts.

To this recipe, we now would like to mix in:

CORE CONCEPT #5:

The Master Mind Alliance enjoys its greatest strength in the diversity of the backgrounds of its members.

This flies in the face of the human tendency to lock only onto similarities and to shut out all differences. For great Master Minding to work, you don't need people who know what you know; you need people with training, insight, disposition and sensibility different from your own.

Let me add something to Walter's remark about meeting David Keener, "It was the first time I connected with someone who brought to the table an entirely different set of assets than I had." This is an understatement. You will not find two people in the world more opposite than these two were.

The ultimate extrovert, Walter is a kinetic hurricane, a vital, charming, lovable guy whose presence compels people; he's like an ambassador to your own potential; the greatest facilitator, he can help take you anywhere you want to go. David, on the other hand,was like a private eye who blends into the scene so thoroughly no one ever notices him. The complete introvert, he could sit next to you on an eight-hour flight and you'd never think to look over at him. But that lack of charisma is only a disguise. Not only would he have noticed you, but were you able to engage him, he could have revealed things about you that even your close friends don't know.

When I first came on board Planned Marketing Associates, I couldn't figure these two out. That is, not until I saw them in action together. It wasn't simply that each covered the other's weakness and multiplied his strengths. Let me put it this way: like Walter's grandmother said, "The human mind is mysterious." In a word, they gave each other *access*. They pooled their mental resources. And the well was deeper than either one of them imagined. Watching Walter and David work together created the sense that whatever these two minds conceive and believe, they could achieve.

By assembling individuals from different fields of expertise, everyone in the group gains from everyone else's skills. Each gets stronger, better and quicker—often in ways that they could not have done on their own. This is the Master Mind Alliance at work.

CORE CONCEPT #6:

The Law of Compensation.

Whether you prefer to think of it as the Golden Rule, "as ye sow, so shall ye reap" or just plain karma, we like to think there is a universal balancing act going on. For our purposes, however, we try to simplify it by saying: *It's impossible to help another without helping yourself.* If you help enough other people get more of what they want and less of what they don't want, you'll never have to worry about getting what you want.

We all know the paradox. **You can't get the loving exchange without giving the loving exchange.** What else ruins marriages? What else drives companies to bankruptcy? What else slows down the magnetic power of your Master Mind Alliance? The selfishness of a me-first mentality! Can greed, anger, jealousy, anxiety, covetousness, injury, "bad luck" and slander be far behind? To keep the law working on our side, the method for getting is giving.

The trouble with a universal law is that it works both ways. So we caution: *Never put yourself in a situation with a Master Mind Alliance where you're getting more than you're giving.* The only way we know to get more for what you do is to give more. If you allow your payback to exceed your contribution, you'll pay for it somewhere down the line.

However, if you continue to give beyond measure, the alliance grows in strength and inspiration. **Since we're essentially talking about the mental, magnetic power of harmonious thinking to produce multiplied results, the greatest benefit does not come to the one for whom the service is rendered; it comes to the one who renders the service.**

HOW TO FORM A MASTERMIND ALLIANCE

A Master Mind Alliance is the coordination of knowledge and effort, in a spirit of harmony, between two or more people, for the attainment of a definite purpose. It is **the power of individual minds focused on the same goal, blending harmoniously to create a third or universal mind, which multiplies effectiveness and produces richer results.**

It provides the vehicle for:

- a trusting environment in which a confidential exchange of ideas can flourish;
- advice and problem-solving on personal and business issues;

- **skill development in the human side of enterprise;**
- **personal growth, collective support, expanded network.**

We're often asked, "How do you form a Master Mind?"

We're inclined to think that, like a farmer, you must first plow the field, then plant the seeds, then water and nurture the plant until it takes root and grows into a strong self-sustaining structure. Be patient. A Master Mind Alliance takes time. We recommend that, rather than "spray and pray," you *cull* the most resourceful people you can find to join. How do you know who to ask?

Start with trust.

1. Make a list of people you know who are headed in the same direction that you are, people with similar values and ambitions. Remember that you are not seeking a mentor, but a peer. Keep an eye out for different strengths. People from varied backgrounds—finance, sales, marketing, management—can provide a wide base of experience.
2. Go through the list with the Six Core Concepts of the Master Mind Alliance fresh in your memory. Select the one best person who fits all the criteria.
3. Talk to that one person about your idea for a Master Mind Alliance. Give him or her this book. The right person will say, "I'm with it. Let's go." If you have to explain, you probably have the wrong person.

4. Once you have the right person, meet with him or her and together select a third member.
5. When the three of you are in complete harmony, search for and vote unanimously on a fourth member and so on until you've found the right number of people to achieve the goals that have brought you into alliance in the first place.
6. Although for most purposes the size of your alliance will most likely be between eight and twelve members, *there is no magic number.* Watch for chemistry. You know it's too small when the range of ideas is too limited; you know it's too large when the group feels too impersonal.
7. If you must err, err by growing your alliance too slowly rather than too quickly.
8. Remember that groups have a lifespan. Some will last for several years and others might not go a year. Part of the reason for this is that objectives change as people grow personally and professionally. Base the success of your Master Mind Alliance not on its longevity, but on how well you accomplish the original purpose for your coming together.

How a Master Mind Alliance develops is the subject of our next appendix.

HOW TO RUN A MASTERMIND ALLIANCE

Master Mind Alliances are like marriages: what works for some is murder on others. In the same way that we would counsel an engaged couple about the uniqueness of their union, how you run your alliance has more to do with listening and responding to each other's needs than it does with referring to a rule book. The point to aim toward is everyone's being in tune and aware of what needs to be done. Then the meetings really run themselves.

Finding out what works and what doesn't is part of the journey to the Master Mind. It is in that spirit that the following ideas are offered. They're meant more as reminders or guidelines than as prescriptions.

1. Commitment

Perfect attendance is the fastest way to develop a Master Mind. Likewise, *punctuality* can really set the mood for a positive exchange. *A willingness to listen with a focused heart and undistracted mind* is a third necessary step. The final preliminary commitment is to *participate fully*, sharing real life experiences rather than offering advice and platitudes.

2. When and Where to Meet

Consistency is the best policy. Meetings should be scheduled in a regular fashion, such as the second Tuesday evening of every month. *Meeting in the same place at the same time for approximately the same amount of time* is also a good idea. This "no surprises" approach will help members protect the alliance from the many other commitments they must juggle. Without even checking their date book, they already know that Tuesday belongs to the Master Mind.

The two largest determiners in choosing a place to meet are *comfort* and *confidentiality*. People need to be able to let their guard down and relax. A living room can be ideal. Other groups may prefer meeting in a roundtable or seminar room at a private club. Open seating is the best arrangement. Small considerations in this regard, like having water, juice, coffee or tea, can be very useful in producing a favorable mood. A minimum of distraction — no phones, no noise from other rooms — is a must.

Once the group congeals, protocol may change. For example, a Master Mind Alliance may choose to allow members to call emergency meetings or they may want to make a retreat together. Others may find it beneficial to have an additional meeting quarterly or annually in which others – either prospective members or family – may be invited.

3. How Often to Meet

Some groups do better meeting once a week than once or twice a month. It all depends upon the group's agenda. One thing that experience universally indicates is that meeting less than once a month creates a problem as the group tends to lose synergy.

THE FIRST MEETING

One way to begin the first meeting is for the moderator to present a brief outline for the evening followed by each member's introducing him or herself to the group. Your name, your specialty, your outside interests and what you hope to gain from the group ought to prove sufficient. The moderator would be wise to ask if anyone has questions after each person's introduction. The first order of business might be for the group to generate its purpose.

Once all are aligned to that purpose, expressions of commitment might follow, such as agreements regarding *attendance, punctuality, support and participation.* The focus for that first night might be what the Master Mind Alliance can do for each member, or, if a certain issue has a common resonance, the group might tackle that. By everyone's sharing their own needs as well as their expertise, the group already begins to think like a Master Mind. The meeting might close with a list of other considerations the group wants to address in subsequent meetings.

FORMAT FOR OTHER MEETINGS

1. Since time is always a factor, the moderator ought to call the meeting to order in a timely fashion.
2. Setting the tone for confidentiality and disclosure, he or she might ask members to deliver, round-robin style, a brief update on what's happened since the last meeting in three areas: personal, family and business. It's best to restrict this to two and half minutes, certainly no longer than five minutes, for each member.
3. After each person has been heard, the moderator selects, with the consensus of the group, two key issues that members have brought up.
4. The member with the key issue elaborates. The group asks questions to get more information. The objective here is not to advise but to *counsel* and invite members to share their own experiences.
5. Finally the group offers *options*, not solutions. Instead of "Do this" the format is more like "What if...."

Some groups like to invite a member to present a topic. Subjects could be of general concern to the group like pricing a new product or how to make a presentation to a bank, or they could be specific to the presenter like uncertainty about firing a key employee or getting a better grip on family finances. Once open for discussion, the moderator must be mindful of what the presenter is looking for in terms of response. "I just want you to listen" is different from "I'm confused and I seek clarity" or "I need advice and real counsel."

Instead of a member's presenting a topic, some groups will invite a specialist to deliver a report specific to the needs of the group. Hiring, for example, one public relations consultant or marketing analyst for one informal evening can prove extremely beneficial for all.

The meeting might end with a wrap-up in which the moderator invites everyone to summarize their thoughts and feelings for the evening and reminds everyone what's to be discussed at the next meeting.

USE OF A MODERATOR

If your Master Mind Alliance is made up of three or more people, you will invariably need a moderator. The job can be rotated so that everyone gets a chance at developing these skills. By moderator, we mean someone assigned to:

- *lead the group through its agenda in a timely manner;*
- *sense the pulse of the group and monitor its progress;*
- *exemplify a spirit of openness;*
- *deliver appropriate feedback;*
- *draw out those members who are stuck, quiet or shy;*
- *maintain order and purpose;*
- *clarify confusions;*
- *help keep everyone's eyes on the prize.*

Undoubtedly, someone with training in human relations and communication skills is a huge plus. For one thing, a moderator with savvy saves a lot of time. The mood of a group can quickly shift from spontaneous, curious and creative to pretentious, deceitful and withholding without anyone's quite knowing why. At the first sign that empathy is degenerating into detachment, indifference or avoidance, the wise moderator can help keep the group on track by demonstrating active listening.

For another thing, a moderator understands that disclosures of a personal nature need an honest, supportive audience. However, people are not always aware when their observations turn judgmental, hostile, critical or preachy. A simple reminder, "We would prefer if you spoke from your own experience," can keep the group collaboratively focused, rather than territorial and competitive.

Furthermore, a moderator accepts the fact that powerful information can threaten even the most secure person. Some material is stashed so far back in the mind that its expression invariably will be ambiguous and hard to follow. Aware of this, the caring moderator can create a climate of permission. Moreover, knowing that arrogance and condescension can wipe out participation and the appreciation of differences, the sensitive moderator will challenge any dogmatic and unfounded assertions, thereby returning the group to an investigative and open-minded position.

In addition, the moderator can maintain the air of confidentiality that is the cornerstone of any Master Mind. This is not to suggest that people intentionally "give up the group," but an inadvertent slip can cause the same damage as an outright betrayal. The moderator begins and ends every session with that most useful of phrases, "What's said in this room stays in this room."

Finally, the crucial task of developing the trust quotient of the group lies with the moderator's ability to release, remind and restrain all the impulses of the members. The role of the moderator is foremost in this regard.

If the group feels that its members lack these skills, they may decide to hire a facilitator. One group determined to learn as much as they could about moderating; each member enrolled in a different course of study, teaching the rest of the group his or her specialty. Learning to be an effective moderator is one of the great by-products of a Master Mind Alliance. Ultimately each member ought to get better and better at the role.

OTHER TIPS

A Master Mind Alliance develops in the same way that a meeting develops. *Start slowly* with nuts and bolts topics which are relatively safe, ones that are not particularly loaded emotionally and whose benefit is clear and distinct. Don't let bad news crowd the group. Too much disclosure too soon can destroy the harmony you're looking to develop. *Trust must be earned over time.* Nothing of lasting emotional significance is going to happen in a single night.

Only when the membership begins to brim with respect for one another, only when friendship is already firmly established can the group allow issues of a more intimate nature to be entertained. At this point, instead of shocking or alienating the members of the alliance, these higher risk topics will invite people to cross over to a more caring and interdependent atmosphere. If people start voting with their feet, that is, they stop coming regularly, you know you've gone too far too quickly.

The last phase of a group – and a meeting – is the one characterized by the contagious sensation called Ready-for-Anything. Only when everyone can say, "I care, you care, we all care," does the invisible power of the Master Mind make itself known.

It is at this juncture that the real magic begins. What is the essence of that magic? **WHATEVER THE HUMAN MIND CAN CONCEIVE AND BELIEVE, IT CAN ACHIEVE.**

MASTER MINDING & BOOT KAMP

Every Planned Marketing seminar – whether for sales people, entrepreneurs, professionals or young people – is a Master Mind Alliance. That's why we give this booklet to attendees, to encourage them to see the wealth of valuable information all around them, not just from the stage or from our staff but from the other attendees as well. In order to get where you are going further and faster, in order to reap the most benefit from the Boot Kamp, we like to encourage each person to bring a Master Mind mentality to the table.

Those who do so inevitably have a more profound experience of what we offer. You might say we at Planned

Marketing deliver the same information, but the connections people make to that information and to one another alter dramatically the outcome of the seminar. Indeed, this is the real secret of this booklet, that by developing the attitude of a Master Mind thinker, another level of one's intelligence comes into play.

Tap into the people around you and ask those individuals for their input. We like to say that a *pure thinker* is less valuable than a *transitional thinker,* someone capable of **sync-ing and linking**, that is, listening to the input of other people and applying their ideas in a new configuration.

We can think of no better way to end the booklet than by sharing a few testimonials sent to us by recent graduates of our seminars. We think their words will prove beneficial, enriching your experience of Boot Kamp while illustrating, by example, the Master Mind principle at work.

I've been around the block a few times and I'm not easily impressed. However, if I had to select one word to describe the CEO Boot Kamp it would be "moving." Knowing the typical seminar game from the inside, I have a keen eye out for insincerity. To anyone about to attend, I want to say that I found instead a rare combination of genuine, down-home compassion with a no-nonsense approach to business.

—Virgil L. Klunder, Founder,
International Locator, Cape Coral FL

To a prospective Boot Kamper, let me only say that I've received more than I ever bargained for—and not just my financial profits, which have increased tremendously. My motivation toward everything else I do in life has risen as well. I've also done away with all forms of procrastination, set written goals that I carry around with me and am bringing my wife and my best friend and his wife to the next seminar. The improvement my life has undergone must be shared.

—Dr. Kal B. Khaled, D.D.S.,
Mississauga ONTARIO (Canada)

I'd heard good things about Planned Marketing, but I never imagined I would learn so much professionally while resolving so much personally. It turned my life around! I had not realized the extent to which unresolved anger had been controlling my business, friendships and marriage. It was such a relief to let it go. I returned home from CEO Boot Kamp a different person.

—Suzanne Droese, President, Inkcorporated,
Dallas TX

My only remark to potential attendees is this: be careful of expectations. Boot Kamp went way beyond my expectations! I brought my whole staff along, from seasoned sales and marketing personnel to new employees. They were thrilled to learn active listening and problem-solving skills while instilling customer trust and increasing their own self-confidence.

—R.J. Girolami, Marketing Operations Manager
Public Service Electric & Gas Company, Newark NJ

When I arrived at my first Eagle University course, I thought I knew everything. I hadn't realized that I was emotionally shut down and really resistant. I always seemed able to find an objection or an exception. It wasn't until I got home that I understood what people had been telling me all along: my ego just wouldn't let go. I treated the seminar like it was some sort of competition I had to win. But after following the advice I got at the course—I wrote my parents with whom I'd been haveing a problem and I volunteered my services to youth in the community—I saw a much bigger world than the size of my mind. When I returned a year later as an intern, my experience of the seminar was enormously enriched. I got out of my head and all the petty distinctions I made. I learned how to participate, not dominate. I learned how to care, not put down people who were different from me. It was as if I had died to the uncaring side of me and found myself reborn in a me I liked a whole lot more. I think this is what changed my life and opened up my career.

—Ryan Mattox, Harvard University, class of '95

What Boot Kamp has given pharmacists is right on target. The whole team shows a keen sensitivity and understanding of what is going on in our profession. Under normal circumstances they have earned our highest commendation and thanks. Under the extenuating circumstances of our last seminar, however, they deserve the additional citation as miracle workers!

—Luther Parker, R.Ph., CAE, Executive Director,
Texas Pharmaceutical Association

Never in my wildest dreams did I think I would be one of those people who would ever write a testimonial. However, so much in my life is changing, so why not this? I took a lot home with me, but two things started working magic immediately. First, I shot all the turkeys in my life that were dragging me down, draining my self-esteem; the joy I feel around eagles is much appreciated. Second, finding, defining and verbalizing my "Magnificent Obsession" has allowed me to start on the path to make it come true. I'd heard of this process before, but this really got me through it. The only counsel I would give a potential Boot Kamper is to let the material touch your life.

—Alice H. Hart, dental spouse, Marietta GA

I never expected to be so blown away! I thought I was coming to a strictly marketing seminar and I ended up leaving a hundred pounds lighter. I didn't realize that the monkeys on my back were so heavy. The only advice I would give a newcomer to your seminar is not to be afraid to ASK.

—Dr. Terry M. Gibson, D.C., Chico CA

Eagle University unites interpersonal skills with real life strategies that work. It made my transition into college so much smoother. I always knew I would succeed; I just didn't know how. The seminar helped me define "focus." Of all the high school graduation gifts I received, this was truly the most valuable. I can't put a price on what it has done for me.

—Ellen Hecht, Penn State, Class of '99

I arrived at Boot Kamp a tired, burned-out skeptic seriously considering a career change. I soon realized it was me, not my career, that needed changing. I expected to learn practical things about dentistry, but the course taught me things even more valuable: how to improve my marriage, how to raise well-balanced children, how to create a million dollar business without spending a fortune, and the greatest gift of all, the art of focusing. It challenged me to change and, in so doing, restored my faith in myself.

—Jayme Tunis, Dental Management Consultant, New Whiteland IN

I've attended just about every type of program offered. What they all have in common is that they are impersonal and the results of attending them are short-lived. The CEO Boot Kamp, however, was what I would call a once-in-a-lifetime experience. It isn't just that business is up over 50% in spite of these lean and mean times. It's more like I can't go back to business as usual.

—Dale R. Reed III, Assistant Vice President, Merrill Lynch, Irving TX

Graduate Dental Boot Kamp put the icing on the cake. Though I gained so much from my first Boot Kamp, what I had failed to get a hold of was the leadership of my own office. For the first time in seven years, I now feel totally in control in a staff meeting. The true secret of success is to find the heart of a patient and not their teeth. Thanks for showing me how to be a leader.

—Dr. Jeffrey Gray, D.D.S., La Mesa CA

What Planned Marketing has put together is the best overall seminar I have ever attended. If there are any chiropractors who have any doubts about investing the time and money, they shouldn't. They should JUST GO! If they're not 100% satisfied with the results, I'll pay for their tuition!

—Dr. David Haggard, D.C., Phoenix AZ

To anyone attending a Boot Kamp, let me tell you what happened to me. First, during the seminar I decided to quit smoking. I had no idea how much control smoking had on my life, especially regarding my family. Second, I wrote down, for the first time in my life, my goals for the year. Within the first three months, I met all thirteen goals. Of course, now I add to them regularly. Third, I stepped out of my comfort zone. I learned conversational Japanese in order to communicate better with our best patients and referrals, most of whom are from Japan. Now the rest of our dental team is learning Japanese as well. Mostly, I feel I am living every day to the fullest.

—Connie Andrews, Novi Family Dental Center, Novi MI

Vici and I have participated in countless seminars, training sessions and sales conventions. This is the best of them all! If anyone truly wants to achieve life enrichment and career fulfillment, going to Boot Kamp is a must. The time and money we invested in order to get the training has generated more returns than we could ever have imagined.

—Dick French, President, Paradigm Communication Company, Monroe LA

My entire staff and I were truly impressed with the plethora of applicable management skills we learned at Boot Kamp, although I must admit that I was skeptical about how well these skills would actually work in the office. The day following the seminar, we met for an all-day staff meeting. The very next day we began to implement the changes and the patients literally cannot get in the door fast enough. I am skeptical no longer! From the way we answer the phone to the way we dialogue with patients, the changes in our office and in the level of motivation of my staff have been outstanding.

—Dr. Diane Marosy, D.D.S., Mena AR

I am a veterinarian in a small town in central Texas, and, even though the average person would not think a seminar on sales and handling people was a necessity, I found it a MUST. I've attended no fewer than five such seminars in the last three years and found Boot Kamp to be the most helpful by far. A conservative estimate is that I've gotten a tenfold return on my investment.

—Dr. Laird Laurence, D.V.M., Fredericksburg, TX

Most seminars are either too "you" intensive or are just shopping lists of closes and techniques. Boot Kamp has the meat. Moreover, I was surrounded by—and have made lasting friendships with—some of the most unique and interesting people I have met in a very long time.

—Larry McIntosh, KLTD 99.1 FM, Austin TX

When I came to Eagle U., I had just turned sixteen and was completely unsure of myself and my talent. However, I came with an open mind. The NEER marketing system was the greatest discovery I have ever made. By applying it, I accomplished my three major goals: to land a role in a Disney feature film ("Camp Nowhere"), to star in a major network TV movie ("The Great American Mom Swap") and to get a part in a TV sit com ("Hang Time"). To anyone about to begin this seminar, I would only paraphrase what was said to me during the course, "Why dream small when you can dream big?"

—Hillary Tuck, Los Angeles CA

YES! Send Me

☐ Information on Planned Marketing's Boot Kamp Seminars **FREE**

☐ Information on Eagle University for Young Adults **FREE**

☐ The Everybody Search Plan **$12.95**

☐ Breaking the NO Barrier **$15.95**

☐ How to Form a MasterMind Alliance **$9.95**

☐ Speak and the Money Will Follow Audio Series **$39.95**

(Plus Shipping)

Name ______ Phone (w/area code)

Shipping Address

City / State / Zip

Signature

Credit card number ☐ Visa ☐ Mastercard ☐ AmEx Exp. Date

Call 800• HUNT•TEX

PLANNED MARKETING ASSOCIATES, INC.

Keep Up with Our Proven Marketing Techniques

☐ **YES!** I am interested in more information on Planned Marketing's Boot Kamp Seminars and other marketing books and products.

Name ______ Phone (w/area code)

Shipping Address

City / State / Zip

PLANNED MARKETING ASSOCIATES, INC.

For our FREE catalog call 800•HUNT•TEX

NO POSTAGE
NECESSARY
IF MAILED
IN THE
UNITED STATES

BUSINESS REPLY MAIL

FIRST-CLASS MAIL PERMIT NO. 300 HUNT TX

POSTAGE WILL BE PAID BY THE ADDRESSEE

Planned Marketing
Publications Division
P.O. Box 345
Hunt TX 78024-9978

NO POSTAGE
NECESSARY
IF MAILED
IN THE
UNITED STATES

BUSINESS REPLY MAIL

FIRST-CLASS MAIL PERMIT NO. 300 HUNT TX

POSTAGE WILL BE PAID BY THE ADDRESSEE

Planned Marketing
Publications Division
P.O. Box 345
Hunt TX 78024-9978